I'll Be PRAYING for You

THOMAS NELSON
Since 1798

I'll Be PRAYING for You

THE LORD GIVES PERFECT *peace* TO THOSE WHOSE *faith* IS FIRM.

—ISAIAH 26:3 CEV

Everything that is done in the world is done by hope.

MARTIN LUTHER

THE LORD
IS MY
STRENGTH AND
MY SHIELD.

—PSALM 28:7

LORD, HELP ME TO

cherish

THESE PRECIOUS DAYS OF TOTAL DEPENDENCY
ON YOU. IT IS EASY TO FORGET
THAT THEY ARE A GIFT, THAT YOU ARE,

day by day,

TEACHING ME TO AWAKEN EVERY MORNING
WITH THIS REQUEST ON MY HEART:
THAT YOU WOULD GRANT ME YOUR

perfect portion

FOR WHATEVER THE DAY HOLDS.

TO REACH THE PORT OF
HEAVEN, WE MUST SAIL
SOMETIMES WITH THE
WIND AND SOMETIMES
AGAINST IT—BUT WE MUST
SAIL, AND NOT DRIFT, NOR
LIE AT ANCHOR.

—OLIVER WENDELL HOLMES

"I am leaving you with a gift—
peace of mind and **heart**.
And the peace I give is a
gift the world cannot give.
So don't be **troubled** or **afraid**."

—JOHN 14:27 NLT

DESIRE ONLY THE WILL OF GOD; SEEK HIM ALONE AND SUPREMELY, AND YOU WILL FIND PEACE.

—FRANÇOIS FÉNELON

O LORD, MY GOD,

MY ONLY HOPE,

HEAR ME,

LEST THROUGH WEARINESS

I SHOULD NOT WISH

TO SEEK YOU. . . .

GIVE ME THE STRENGTH

TO SEEK,

YOU WHO HAVE
CAUSED ME TO FIND YOU,
AND HAVE GIVEN ME
THE HOPE OF FINDING YOU
MORE AND MORE.

—AUGUSTINE

Open your
heart
to hope.

Thank You, Father, for friends who uplift, encourage, support, and pray for me when I don't know how to pray. They are an embodiment of Romans 12:12—"Rejoice in hope, be patient in tribulation, be constant in prayer" (ESV).

Please shape me into this
kind of *prayer warrior*
for others.

No eye has seen,
nor ear heard,
nor the heart of
man imagined,
what God has
prepared for those
who love him.

—1 Corinthians 2:9 ESV

The steadfast love of the LORD never
ceases; his mercies never come to an
end; they are new every morning.

Lamentations 3:22–23 ESV

DON'T TRUST TO HOLD
GOD'S HAND;
LET HIM DO THE
HOLDING, AND YOU
the TRUSTING.
—HAMMER WILLIAM
WEBB-PEPLOE

When you pass through
the waters, I will be
with you; and through the rivers,
they shall not overflow you.
When you walk through the fire,
you shall not be burned,
nor shall the flame scorch you.

—ISAIAH 43:2 NKJV

Never doubt what one prayer can do.

Peace does not
mean to be in a place where
there is no noise, trouble, or
hard work. It means to be in the
midst of all those things and
still be *calm* in your heart.

—*unknown*

FAITH IN A
prayer-hearing
GOD WILL MAKE A
prayer-loving
CHRISTIAN.

—ANDREW MURRAY

He gives **POWER** to the **WEAK**, and to those who have no might He increases **STRENGTH.**

ISAIAH 40:29 NKJV

Thank You, Lord,
for the life You've given us.
As I practice lifting
my face to You in
joyful gladness
each day, I glimpse a
little more freshly that
life here on your
beautiful earth
holds no value without
You as my Center.

Let the words of my mouth
and the meditation of my heart
be acceptable in your sight,
O LORD, my rock and my redeemer.

—Psalm 19:14 ESV

Whenever I am *afraid*, I will *trust* in You. In God (I will *praise* His word), in God I have put my trust; I will not *fear.* What can flesh do to me? . . . In God I have put my trust; I will not be afraid. What can *man* do to me?

—PSALM 56:3–4, 11 NKJV

NO ONE CAN BELIEVE HOW
POWERFUL PRAYER IS AND WHAT IT
CAN EFFECT, EXCEPT THOSE WHO
HAVE LEARNED IT BY EXPERIENCE.
WHENEVER I HAVE PRAYED
EARNESTLY, I HAVE BEEN HEARD
AND HAVE OBTAINED MORE THAN
I PRAYED FOR. GOD SOMETIMES
DELAYS, BUT HE ALWAYS COMES.

· MARTIN LUTHER ·

WHEN I CANNOT
READ, WHEN I
CANNOT THINK,
WHEN I CANNOT
EVEN PRAY,
I CAN TRUST.

• J. HUDSON TAYLOR •

WONDERFUL COUNSELOR,
MIGHTY GOD,
EVERLASTING FATHER,
PRINCE OF PEACE.

ISAIAH 9:6

The greatest answer to

PRAYER is that I am

brought into a

PERFECT understanding

with GOD, and that alters

my view of actual things.

—*Oswald Chambers*

FOUR THINGS LET
US EVER KEEP IN MIND:
GOD HEARS PRAYER,
GOD HEEDS PRAYER, GOD
ANSWERS PRAYER,
AND GOD DELIVERS BY
PRAYER.

–E. M. BOUNDS

START
EACH
day

WITH *a* GRATEFUL *heart.*

PRAYER IS THE BREATH OF THE NEW CREATURE.

—RICHARD BAXTER

I love You, JESUS.
Help me to love You
more and more, to trust
You more and more,
to listen ever more
keenly to Your voice.

DO NOT BE
AFRAID OF *tomorrow,*
FOR GOD IS
ALREADY THERE.

Father, Your Word
says that times
of tribulation are
opportunities to grow
in Christ. Help me
to learn and grow
through this time,
remembering that

"the testing of [my] faith
produces endurance.
And let endurance
have its perfect result,
so that [I] may be
perfect and complete,
lacking in nothing"

(James 1:3–4 NASB).

O *Lord* my God,
teach my *heart* this day
where and how
to *see* You,
where and how
to *find* You.

ST. ANSELM

The LORD will fight
for you; you need
only to be still.
—Exodus 14:14

PRAYER is the natural and joyous breathing of the *spiritual* life by which the heavenly atmosphere is inhaled and then exhaled in prayer.

–Andrew Murray

Lord, I FIND COMFORT IN KNOWING THAT YOU ALONE CAN GIVE ME *peace* THAT *surpasses* MY UNDERSTANDING. I REST IN THAT KNOWLEDGE, TAKE *solace* IN IT, TRUST YOU FOR IT.

MY GRACE IS SUFFICIENT FOR YOU.

2 CORINTHIANS 12:9

Joy is *balm* and
healing, and if you
will but *rejoice*,
God will give *power*.

A. B. SIMPSON

LIKE BURNING INCENSE, LORD, LET MY PRAYER RISE UP TO YOU.

FROM PSALM 141:2

HE SHALL GIVE
HIS ANGELS
CHARGE OVER
YOU, TO KEEP
YOU IN ALL
YOUR WAYS.

PSALM 91:11 NKJV

GOD'S STRENGTH > MY WEAKNESS

Pray the largest prayers. You cannot think a prayer so large that God, in answering it, will not wish you had made it larger. Pray not for crutches but for wings.

PHILLIPS BROOKS

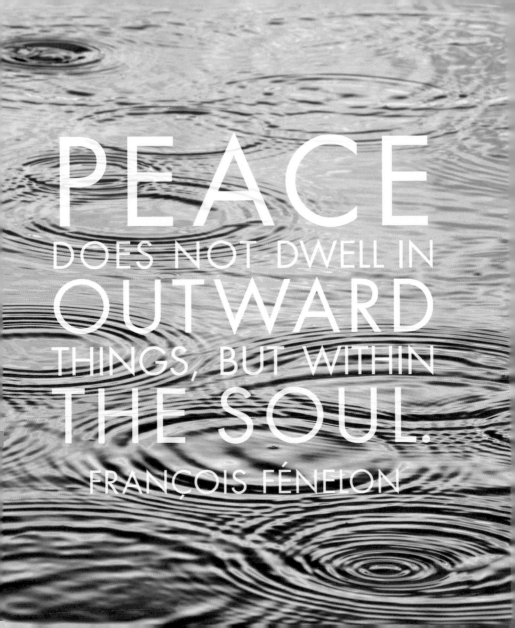

The
Lord is
my shepherd;
there is
nothing
I lack.
from Psalm 23:1

Lord, I need You.
My *desire* is
to *glorify* You, but I
am incapable of doing that
through *my own* effort. Please
bear me up and give me Your
strength. Lift my head
and help me to *rejoice* in You.

LIVE
EACH
DAY
WITH
GRATITUDE . . .

You have redeemed me, O Lord God of truth.

PSALM 31:5 NKJV

The Lord is my rock,
and my fortress,
and my deliverer;
the God of my rock;
in Him I will trust.

2 Samuel 22:2-3 NKJV

God will answer your prayers better than you think. Of course, one will not always get exactly what he has asked for. . . . We all have sorrows and disappointments, but

one must never forget
that, if commended to
God, they will issue in
good. . . . His own
solution is far better
than any we could conceive.

—Fanny J. Crosby

Prayer should be the means
by which I, at all times, receive
all that I need, and, for this
reason, be my daily *refuge*,
my daily *consolation*, my
daily *joy*, my source of rich and
inexhaustible joy in life.

—John Chrysostom

HOLD on to HOPE.

from Romans 12:12

We know not
what prayer
can do.

—Charles Spurgeon

THE JOY OF THE LORD IS YOUR STRENGTH.

—Nehemiah 8:10

Grant me, O Lord my God,
a mind to know you, a heart
to seek you, wisdom to find
you, conduct pleasing to you,
faithful perseverance in waiting
for you, and a hope of finally
embracing you. Amen.

Thomas Aquinas

Lord, You are my *stronghold*.

I envision myself clinging to You during

this season of pain and uncertainty. You

are my ROCK, my REFUGE. When

everything around me seems to be falling

apart, I know that You have me right

where You want me . . . and I trust You.

LORD,

KEEP

MY HEART

WITH YOU.

LORD, REMIND ME THAT
THIS PAIN I FEEL IS ONLY
TEMPORARY AND THAT
YOU WILL ONE DAY "WIPE
AWAY EVERY TEAR FROM
[MY] EYES; AND THERE
WILL NO LONGER BE ANY
DEATH; THERE WILL NO
LONGER BE ANY MOURNING,
OR CRYING, OR PAIN"
(REVELATION 21:4 NASB).

"I will not cause pain without allowing something new to be born," says the LORD.

Isaiah 66:9 NCV

Hope
is the word
which
God has
written on
the brow of
every man.
—Victor Hugo

"HAVE I NOT COMMANDED YOU? BE *strong* AND *courageous.* DO NOT BE FRIGHTENED, AND DO NOT BE *dismayed,* *for the* LORD YOUR GOD IS WITH YOU WHEREVER YOU GO."

—JOSHUA 1:9 ESV

DO WHAT YOU CAN and PRAY FOR WHAT YOU CANNOT YET DO.

—AUGUSTINE

BE STRONG AND
COURAGEOUS. DO NOT
FEAR . . . FOR IT IS THE LORD
YOUR GOD WHO GOES WITH
YOU. HE WILL NOT LEAVE
YOU OR FORSAKE YOU.

—DEUTERONOMY 31:6 ESV

Lord, make me an instrument of thy peace.

FRANCIS OF ASSISI

Lord, I am confused by
the circumstances of my
life right now. Please give
me Your wisdom. As I walk
through this trial, please
teach me what You want
me to learn.

Help me to *lean* on
You every step of the way.

YOUR WAYS,
O LORD,
MAKE KNOWN
TO ME.
TEACH ME
YOUR PATHS.
GUIDE ME
IN YOUR TRUTH
AND TEACH ME,
FOR YOU ARE
GOD MY SAVIOR,
AND FOR YOU
I WAIT
ALL THE DAY

—FROM PSALM 25:4–5

LORD
JESUS . . .
MAY I
CLING TO
NOTHING
BUT TO
YOU.

True faith, by a mighty effort of the will, fixes its gaze on our Divine Helper. . . . It is wisdom and peace to say, "I will trust and not be afraid."

Alexander MacLaren

We have peace
with God through our
Lord Jesus Christ.

Romans 5:1

You share Your **goodness** with those who make You their **sanctuary.**

Psalm 31:19 THE VOICE

The Lord has heard my cry for mercy; the Lord accepts my prayer.

—PSALM 6:9

Hope itself is
like a star—not
to be seen in the
sunshine of
prosperity, and only
to be discovered in the
night of adversity.
—Charles Spurgeon

Father, I am so glad that You
encourage—nay, command me
to cast my burdens on You. Your
shoulders are broad and strong, and far
more capable of carrying what troubles
me. Thank You for instructing me in
Your Word to lay my burdens at Your
feet, and to exchange them
for Your yoke, which is light and easy.

EVERY DAY
I WILL
BLESS YOU,
AND I WILL
PRAISE
YOUR NAME
FOREVER
AND
EVER.

—PSALM 145:2 NASB

Prayer is beyond
any question the
highest activity of
the human soul. Man
is at his greatest and
highest when upon his
knees he comes face
to face with God.

—D. Martyn Lloyd-Jones

IT IS NOT ONLY
OUR DUTY TO PRAY
FOR OTHERS, BUT
ALSO TO DESIRE THE
PRAYERS OF OTHERS
FOR OURSELVES.

William Gurnall

Look to the LORD
and his strength;
seek his face always.
–Psalm 105:4

Lord, right now I feel so overwhelmed.
Help me to rest in you. Help me to
remember that You love me, that You are
with me even in my deepest heartaches.
Help me to remember Your promise that
nothing "will be able to separate [me]
from the love of God, which is in Christ
Jesus our Lord" (Romans 8:39 NASB).

Never was a faithful
prayer lost. Some prayers
have a longer voyage
than others, but then
they return with their
richer lading at last,
so that the praying
soul is a gainer by
waiting for an answer.

—William Gurnall

HE WILL COVER YOU WITH HIS FEATHERS,
AND UNDER HIS WINGS YOU WILL FIND REFUGE.

— *Psalm 91:4*

To fall in love with God is the *greatest* of all romances; to seek him, the greatest *adventure*; to find him, the greatest human achievement.

—Augustine

For the Eternal is always there to protect you.

He will safeguard your each and every step.

Proverbs 3:26 THE VOICE

PRAYER IS NOT OVERCOMING GOD'S RELUCTANCE, BUT LAYING HOLD OF HIS WILLINGNESS.

MARTIN LUTHER

The Lord stood with me and gave me strength.

2 TIMOTHY 4:17 NLT

THY WAY, NOT MINE,
O LORD, HOWEVER
DARK IT BE; LEAD
ME BY THINE OWN
HAND; CHOOSE OUT
THE PATH FOR ME.

Horatius Bonar

Each time, before you
intercede, be quiet first, and
worship God in His glory. Think
of what He can do, and how
He delights to hear the prayers
of His redeemed people. Think
of your place and privilege in
Christ, and expect great things!

—Andrew Murray

Lord, THANK YOU FOR THE PRIVILEGE OF PERSONAL RELATIONSHIP WITH YOU. HELP ME NOT TO TAKE FOR GRANTED THE *awe-inspiring* RIGHT I HAVE AS YOUR CHILD: TO *run* TO YOU, TO BE *held* TIGHT, TO BE *cradled* LOVINGLY IN YOUR ARMS.

HOPE ANCHORS *the* SOUL.

from Hebrews 6:19

Prayer is an
acknowledgment
that our need of
God's help is not
partial but total.

—Alistair Begg

To persist in prayer
without returns,
this is not time lost,
but a great gain.
It is endeavour
without thought
of self
and only
for the glory
of the Lord.

St. Teresa of Avila

As for
me, I will
always
have
hope.

—*Psalm 71:14*

The prayer that begins with trustfulness, and passes on into waiting, will always end in thankfulness, triumph, and praise.

—Alexander MacLaren

Lord, I'm struggling to remember that everything I experience is a gift from You, intended to do me good, not harm. It doesn't feel that way right now, but I long to be restored to that place of comfort and trust, where I know You have me exactly where You want me. I give myself to You now as my center, my focus, my true north. Thank You for never changing.

Seek to cultivate a buoyant, joyous sense of the crowded kindnesses of God in your daily life.

—Alexander MacLaren

YOU NEED NOT CRY VERY LOUD; HE IS NEARER TO US THAN WE THINK.

BROTHER LAWRENCE

IF GOD IS FOR US, WHO CAN BE AGAINST US?

Romans 8:31

"BE
ALWAYS
ON THE
WATCH, AND
PRAY . . . "
LUKE 21:36

Time spent
in *prayer* is
never wasted.

—François Fénelon

⸜✦⸝

Heavenly Father,

I know Your Word promises

that You will never leave me, never

forsake me, but right now I am feeling

alone and forgotten. Please renew me.

Refresh me. Help me to sense Your

presence once again. Help me to rejoice

in Your love and rest in Your grace.

⸜✦⸝

Our whole being must be in our praying.

E.M. BOUNDS

THE BEST AND SWEETEST
FLOWERS OF PARADISE
GOD GIVES TO HIS PEOPLE
WHEN THEY ARE UPON
THEIR KNEES. PRAYER IS
THE GATE OF HEAVEN.

Thomas Brooks

Dear Lord, thank You for the gentle reminder that this life is temporary—and so are difficult circumstances. It is easy to feel overwhelmed because this life is all I know. Help me lift my eyes to You, from where my help comes (Psalm 121:1).

*In all things it
is better to hope
than despair.*

—*Johann Wolfgang von Goethe*

I find rest
in God;
only he gives
me hope.

—Psalm 62:5 NCV

My *times* are in Your hands, *O Lord.* I praise You.

"Be still, and know that I am God."

—Psalm 46:10